Also by Louis Phillips

How Do You Get a Horse out of the Bathtub?
Profound Answers to Preposterous Questions

263 Brain Busters
Just How Smart Are You, Anyway?

Sportsathon
(with Vic Braden)

Haunted House Jokes

Going Ape
Jokes from the Jungle

How Do You Lift a Walrus with One Hand?
More Profound Answers to Preposterous Questions

Way Out!
Jokes from Outer Space

Wackysaurus
Dinosaur Jokes

Invisible Oink
Pig Jokes

School Daze
Jokes Your Teacher Will Hate

KEEP 'EM LAUGHING

JOKES TO AMUSE AND ANNOY YOUR FRIENDS

By Louis Phillips
Illustrated by Michael Chesworth

VIKING

For Joan, Alan, Scott, and Dennis Kramer
(Don't blame me if you don't get laughs)
— L. P.

VIKING
Published by the Penguin Group
Penguin Books USA Inc., 375 Hudson Street, New York, New York 10014, U.S.A.
Penguin Books Ltd, 27 Wrights Lane, London W8 5TZ, England
Penguin Books Australia Ltd, Ringwood, Victoria, Australia
Penguin Books Canada Ltd, 10 Alcorn Avenue, Toronto, Ontario, Canada M4V 3B2
Penguin Books (N.Z.) Ltd, 182–190 Wairau Road, Auckland 10, New Zealand

Penguin Books Ltd, Registered Offices: Harmondsworth, Middlesex, England

First published in 1996 by Viking, a division of Penguin Books USA Inc.

1   3   5   7   9   10   8   6   4   2

Text copyright © Louis Phillips, 1996
Illustrations copyright © Michael Chesworth, 1996
All rights reserved

LIBRARY OF CONGRESS CATALOGING-IN-PUBLICATION DATA
Phillips, Louis.
Keep 'em laughing : jokes to amuse and annoy your friends /
by Louis Phillips ; illustrated by Michael Chesworth.   p.   cm.
Summary: A collection of jokes, puns, knock-knock jokes, and riddles.
ISBN 0-670-86009-3
1. Wit and humor, Juvenile.   2. Riddles, Juvenile.   [1. Wit and humor
2. Riddles.   3. Jokes.]   I. Chesworth, Michael, ill.   II. Title.
PN6163.P498 1996   818'.5402—dc20 95-23734 CIP AC

Printed in USA
Set in New Century Schoolbook

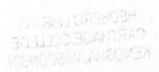

RYAN: Why did the bubble gum cross the road?
BOBBY: It was stuck to the chicken's foot.

Knock, knock.
Who's there?
Juicy.
Juicy who?
Juicy the new video on MTV?

NICOLE: Is that a real diamond ring you're wearing?
TONI: If it isn't, I've just been gypped out of twenty-
        nine cents.

EYE DOCTOR: Would you please read the third row
on that chart on the wall?
PATIENT: What chart?

DEBORAH: What is creamy, light brown, full of
peanuts, and deadly?
CHAIM: What?
DEBORAH: Shark-infested peanut butter.

MOM: Turn the car around. I forgot to unplug the
iron.

DAD: Don't panic. The house won't burn down. I forgot to turn off the shower.

TEACHER: What did you write your report on?
IAN: A piece of paper.

MICHAEL: They say you're going to open a bakery.
RHONA: If I can raise the dough.

NEIGHBOR: Hey, Fred, are you using your lawn
mower this afternoon?
FRED *(who is tired of his neighbor always borrowing
things)*: Yes, I am.
NEIGHBOR: Great! Then you won't be using your golf
clubs. Can I borrow them?

POST OFFICE CLERK: This package is too heavy.
You'll have to put another stamp on it.
MONA: And putting another stamp on it will make it
lighter?

CARPENTER: Why are you leaving work so early?
ASSISTANT: I'm not. I'm making a bolt for the door.

JOHN: My uncle was kicked out of the submarine service.

GINNY: What did he do?

JOHN: He insisted on sleeping with the windows open.

MATTHEW WASSERMAN: What is it you throw out when you need it and take back when you don't?

MARVIN: What?

MATTHEW WASSERMAN: An anchor.

Knock, knock.
Who's there?
Tarzan.
Tarzan who?
Tarzan stripes forever.

PAT: Were you ever in a play?
MIKE: No, but my foot was in a cast.

NANCY: Here I am, bright and early.
LAUREN: Well, at least you're early.

The telephone rings.
"Hello."
"Hi."
"That you, Joe?"
"This is Joe."
"You don't sound like Joe."
"This is Joe, all right."
"Are you sure?"
"Of course I'm sure."
"Well, Joe, this is Al."
"Hi, Al."
"I was wondering if you could loan me a thousand
    dollars for a month or so."
"I'll tell Joe you called when he comes in."

BOB: How can I make a strawberry shake?
MARGIE: Take it to see a horror movie.

KEN HOLMES: How do you make an elephant float?
BURNHAM: I don't know, how?
KEN HOLMES: Well, you take some soda water, then add two scoops of ice cream and one elephant.

JOHN: Does the invisible man have any children?
AMY: How could he? He's not apparent.

SAM: It took me ten years to compose this lullaby.
BART: Perhaps you should have used a computer.
SAM: But I did use a computer.
BART: Then how come it took you so long?
SAM: It kept putting me to sleep.

ZACHARY: What's the difference between a fish and a piano?
ERIC: What?
ZACHARY: You can tune a piano but you can't tuna fish.

ALAN: What's a knob?
JAMIE: Just another thing to adore.

NANCY: What did dinosaurs use to decorate their bathroom walls?

LAUREN: What?

NANCY: Rep-tiles.

RACHEL: What happened when a skunk, a female deer, and a duck went out to eat at a fancy restaurant?

DEBORAH: I haven't the foggiest idea.

RACHEL: The skunk had only a scent and the deer had only one buck, so the cost of the meal ended up on the duck's bill.

Boss: Tell me where you've worked before.
Employee: The Sahara Forest. I was a lumberjack.
Boss: Wait a minute! The Sahara is a desert. There are no trees there.
Employee: See how well I did my job?

Son: Mom, what's a werewolf?
Mother: Be quiet and comb your face.

Boy (running home from nursery school): Mom, Mom, guess what? Today I learned how to count.
Mom: Let me hear you.
Boy: One, two, three.
Mom: Go on.
Boy: You mean there's more?

JANE: Do you know the capital of Alaska?

MEDWICK: Juneau?

JANE: Of course I know, but I'm asking you.

PIANO TEACHER: What do you get if a child stands under a falling piano?

YOUNG STUDENT: I don't know, what?

PIANO TEACHER: You get A flat minor.

ALEX MALLORY: Can you telephone from your car?

MICHAEL MALLORY: Of course I can tell a phone from my car. My car is much larger.

DAVID: Why didn't the cannibal eat the circus clown after boiling him alive?

BILL: Why?

DAVID: Because he tasted funny.

MICHAEL: What kind of school do you have to drop out of to graduate?

ALEX: What kind?

MICHAEL: Parachute school, of course.

JOAN: You remind me of the ocean.

ALBERT: Because I'm wild, romantic, and restless?

JOAN: No, because you make me sick to my stomach.

A peanut sat on a railroad track,
His heart was all aflutter.
Around the bend came a choo-choo train,
Toot, toot! Peanut butter.

EILEEN: What do you call a masked man who works at the bank?
SARAH: What?
EILEEN: The loan arranger.

MICKEY: What happened when all the king's men played a practical joke on Humpty-Dumpty?
RIZZUTO: What?
MICKEY: He fell for it.

ALBERT: You're not going to play poker with Brewer, are you?
HERMAN: Of course I am.
ALBERT: But Brewer has a reputation for cheating.
HERMAN: No, last time we played, he beat me fair and square. He had four aces and I only had three.

AUNT AMY: Why are you staring so hard at that orange juice carton?
IAN: Because it says "concentrate."

Can February March? No, but April May.

A tourist in Texas walked into the largest hotel he had ever seen. "My name is Perry Gold, I've been driving for twelve hours straight, I'm exhausted, and I have a reservation. Can you please tell me what room I'm in?"

"Certainly, sir," the desk clerk said. "You're in the lobby."

Knock, knock.
Who's there?
Butcher.
Butcher who?
Butcher arms
    around me
    and give me a
    little kiss.

DOCTOR: Just remember.
    Plenty of exercise
    will kill germs.
PATIENT: Great. How do
    I get the germs to
    exercise?

PATIENT: Doctor, I am very depressed. I don't know what to do with myself.

DOCTOR: I suggest you throw yourself into your work.

PATIENT: But, Doctor, I mix concrete!

JAMES: I woke up last Thursday night and I thought my watch was gone.

PAUL: And was it?

JAMES: No, but it was going.

EVERETT: What were your three most difficult years in school?
MELVIN: Second grade.

LESLIE: What is Bugs Bunny's least favorite dessert?
LORNA: What?
LESLIE: Elmer Fudge.

Knock, knock.
Who's there?
Beats me. I forgot my name.

Knock, knock.
Who's there?
Snow.
Snow who?
Snow use in asking. I still can't remember my name.

LOIS: Do you know the duke of Friage? He's the biggest snob I know.
ADAM: How snobbish is he?
LOIS: He's so snobbish he won't even ride in the same car with his chauffeur.

RACHEL: What do you get if you cross a cheetah with a centipede?

ADAM: What?

RACHEL: An animal that can outrun all the other animals, but takes all day to get its sneakers on.

What do you call a large white whale that lies at the bottom of the sea but can't seem to make up its mind?

Maybe Dick.

WISE GUY #1: Hiya, stupid.

WISE GUY #2: I didn't come here to be insulted.

WISE GUY #1: No? Where do you usually go?

JUGGLER: Look here, I object to going on right after the monkey act.

MANAGER: You're right. The audience might think you're an encore.

TEACHER: Tristan, how would you punctuate the following sentence? As I was walking along the street, I saw a hundred-dollar bill lying on the sidewalk.

TRISTAN: I would make a dash after it.

The principal of a local high school went downstairs to visit the janitor. When he entered the basement, the principal was astonished to see the janitor seated at a low, small table playing chess with his dog.

"Sam, that's a pretty smart dog you have there," the principal said. "I've never seen a dog play chess before."

The janitor looked up. "Oh, this dog's not so smart. I've beaten him three out of five games so far."

SON: Dad, can I go out and play?
FATHER: What, with all those holes in your pants?
SON: No, with the kids next door.

BULLETIN BOARDS ARE TACKY.

SON *(on a family trip):* Dad, you had better pick up
that heavy trunk. Grandpa won't like it lying
there.
DAD: Where is Grandpa?
SON: Under the trunk.

CONNIE: What's the difference between a prison
guard and a person with measles?
RICHARD: What?
CONNIE: One spots breakouts, while the other
breaks out in spots.

An Englishman parachuted from a plane and landed in the outback of Australia. A native approached.

"Pardon me," the Englishman asked politely, "but do you speak English?"

"Tweet, buzz eek-squawk, yes," the native answered.

"May I ask your name?"

"Oooeee squee-awwk buzz, Morford," came the reply.

"And tell me, just where did you learn to speak English?"

"Tweet buzz wheeoooo, click-buzz. From short-wave radio."

TRISTAN: What's the difference between?
LAURIE: Between what?
TRISTAN: I'm not giving any hints.

VOICE ON THE OTHER END OF THE PHONE: Pardon me, is this five five five twenty-two twenty-two?
DEXTER: Sorry, you must have the wrong number. This is five five five two two two two.

JOHN: Drat! This match won't light.
SAM: Maybe it's wet.
JOHN: No, it's not. I just lit it a few minutes ago.

ANDREW: My father climbed Mount Everest. Now,
    that's a foot to be proud of.
NORMAN: Don't you mean *feat*?
ANDREW: No. He only climbed it once.

Knock, knock.
Who's there?
Repeat.
Repeat who?
Okay. Who who who who who . . .

Show me a home where the buffalo roam, and I'll
show you a messy house!

DOCTOR: How can I help you?

PATIENT: I'm having trouble breathing.

DOCTOR: Well, I can give you something to stop that.

The opera singer was bragging to the orchestra conductor:

OPERA SINGER: I hope you noticed the other night how my great tenor voice filled the hall.

CONDUCTOR: Of course I noticed. Everybody was getting up and leaving to make room for it.

ONE MIND READER TO ANOTHER: What's new? As if I don't already know.

ONE MIND READER TO ANOTHER: You're fine. How am I?

MESSAGE ON THE MIND READER'S ANSWERING MACHINE: No need to leave your name, number, or a brief message. I'll call you back when I return.

RACHEL: No.

DEBORAH: Do you believe in mind reading?

PAUL: What do frogs do after they're married?

NATALIE: What?

PAUL: They live hoppily ever after.

STEVEN: What do you call a line of cabs waiting outside the Dallas airport?
ROCHELLE: What?
STEVEN: The Yellow Rows of Taxis.

A young woman approached the desk clerk of a prominent hotel. "I beg your pardon, sir," she inquired, "but is there a man staying here with one eye named Bobby Hoffman?"

"I don't know," the clerk replied. "What's the name of his other eye?"

Knock, knock, knock, knock, knock, knock, knock, knock.
Who's there?
John the Octopus.

A college professor went into a drugstore and approached the druggist:
PROFESSOR: I would like some prepared acetyl derivative of salicylic acid, please.
DRUGGIST: Do you mean aspirin?
PROFESSOR: Yes. I can never remember that name.

ONE CAMEL TO ANOTHER: I don't care what anybody says. I'm thirsty.

A young boy entered the ice-cream parlor. He saw a genie standing behind the soda fountain. "Wow!" the young boy exclaimed. "Are you really a genie?"

"I am."

"And you work here behind the soda fountain?"

"Yes. What do you want?"

"Make me a milk shake."

"Okay," the genie replied. "ZAP! You're a milk shake."

TOM: Sometimes a person can be too polite.

JOANNE: How is that possible?

TOM: Well, I knew a deep-sea diver. He was out walking on the bottom of the ocean when he saw a mermaid. He tipped his hat to her and drowned.

JOHN: Why is our friend Ben Hamalianopodiolis changing his name?
LAWYER: Hard to say.

Knock, scratch.
Who's there?
Captain Hook.

ASTRONOMER: Now, tell me. Which is more important—the sun or the moon?
HARRIET: The moon.
ASTRONOMER: How can you say that?
HARRIET: Easy. The moon gives us light at night, when we need it. The sun gives us light only during the day, when we don't need it.

SERGEANT: All right, Private Amherst. I called, "Company, halt!" and everybody came to a dead stop. Everybody but you, knucklehead. Why not?
PRIVATE: Well, Sarge, I've been part of this platoon for so long, I didn't feel I was company any longer.

KAY: A dog bit my leg.
DOCTOR: Did you put something on it?
KAY: No, the dog liked it just the way it was.

POET: I put my whole mind into that poem.
EDITOR: Blank verse, I suppose.

ARNIE: Can you say "iced ink" five times fast?
ED: Iced ink, iced ink, iced ink, iced ink, iced ink.
ARNIE: Well, if you stink, why don't you take a bath?

CHRISTOPHER: What's the difference between Santa
    Claus and a warm dog?
JOANNE: What?
CHRISTOPHER: Santa Claus wears a red suit. The dog
    just pants.

PASSENGER: Driver, will this bus take me to
    Broadway?
BUS DRIVER: Upper or lower?
PASSENGER: All of me, I hope.

ONE FROG TO ANOTHER: Time sure is fun when
    you're having flies.

MARYHELEN: After Minnie Mouse fell into the river,
    how did Mickey Mouse revive her?
CAROLINE: How?
MARYHELEN: He used mouse-to-mouse resuscitation.

In twenty years of work, Albert had never been late—not once. But then one morning, the clock struck nine and there was no Albert. Twenty minutes passed. An hour. Two hours. Finally, at noon, the door to the office opened, and in walked Albert. His arm was in a sling, his head was bandaged, and he was walking on crutches.

His boss ran up to him. "Albert! What happened to you? We were worried."

"I'm sorry, boss. I fell down a flight of stairs."

"It took you three hours to fall down a flight of stairs?"

LAURIE: What's orange and stands 102 stories high?
J.P.: What?
LAURIE: The Empire State Carrot.

J.P.: What building in New York City does Dracula
   like to visit?
LAURIE: What?
J.P.: The Vampire State Building.

MATTHEW: Could Noah read on the ark at night?
JAKE: Sure, he had floodlights.

ERNIE: Why are you throwing all those nails away?
JOEL: Because the points are facing in the wrong
    direction.
ERNIE: Perhaps they were meant to be used on the
    other side of the house.

There was a very powerful ruler in India, and this
ruler loved tigers. He loved them so much that he
refused to allow any of his subjects to shoot a tiger
under any conditions whatsoever. Pretty soon, the
tigers were overrunning the village and devouring
the citizens.

Day after day, the citizens pleaded with the
mighty ruler. "Oh please, Maharaja, allow us to kill
some of the tigers before they eat us all," they
begged. But the maharaja refused to listen to their
pleas.

"No tiger will be killed as long as I am the
ruler," he insisted.

Finally the citizens, in desperation, overthrew
the maharaja and placed a new ruler upon the
throne.

*It was the first time in history that the reign was
called because of game.*

EDITH: I need to find seventeen friends to go to the movie with me.

ANDY: Why?

EDITH: Because the sign out front said UNDER 18 NOT ADMITTED

FIRST KANGAROO: What's the matter?

SECOND KANGAROO: I don't know. I feel jumpy today.

Joan came home and saw that her younger sister was in tears.

"What are you crying about?" Joan asked her sister.

"I'm crying," Karen replied, "because I cleaned the birdcage and the bird disappeared."

"How did that happen?"

"I cleaned the cage with a vacuum cleaner."

NELSON BREEN: In what way are elephants and pickles alike?

ALEX: I give up.

NELSON BREEN: They're both green—except, of course, for the elephant.

What's purple, dangerous, and goes up and down?

A grape with a machine gun inside an elevator.

ALEX: What's gray, has long, silvery wings, and
    brings money to elephants?
DANA: What?
ALEX: The Tusk Fairy.

TEACHER: Tell me, Tommy. Who was Homer?
TOMMY: He was the guy Babe Ruth made famous.

ANDREW KATZ: Why did the traffic light turn red?
OLIVIA KATZ: Why?
ANDREW KATZ: It was embarrassed at having to
    change in front of so many people.

A man named Amos went to buy a horse, but the owner didn't want to sell it to him.

"Why are you so reluctant to sell this horse?" Amos inquired.

"Well, to be honest with you, this horse is very strange. He recognizes only two commands. When you want him to run as fast as the wind, you have to say, 'Thank goodness!' But when you want him to stop, you have to say, 'Tom Cruise!'"

"That sounds easy enough," Amos said. "Let me try it out. If I like my ride, I'll pay you $20,000 for him."

"Fair enough."

And so Amos got on the horse. "Thank goodness," he said, and the horse took off as fast as the wind. The horse tore across the open plains and up the mountains. After a while, though, Amos wanted the horse to stop, but he couldn't remember the name. "John Wayne!" he cried. Still the horse kept on running—but now they were heading straight for the edge of a cliff. The drop was several hundred feet. "Dolly Parton, Cary Grant, Bill Clinton!" he yelled. Still the horse ran on.

When the horse was only two feet from the edge of the cliff, Amos remembered the name. "Tom Cruise!" he cried. The horse stopped running, just in the nick of time.

As Amos sat on his horse at the edge of the cliff, peering down into the canyon, he wiped his brow with his handkerchief.

"Thank goodness!" he said.

PETER: What's the difference between a rhinoceros and a chocolate chip cookie?
JENNY: What?
PETER: It's very difficult to dunk a rhino in your milk.

PATRICK: What do you get when you cross a kangaroo with an elephant?
LUCAS: What?
PATRICK: Potholes all over Australia.

RYAN: Look at all those flies around the basketball field.

BOBBY: Why don't you shoo them?

RYAN: Naah. Let them go barefoot like the rest of the bugs.

JENNIFER: I'm so upset. I just made supper for the whole family, and our cat jumped up on the table and ate it.

JASON: Don't worry, sis. Mom will get us a new cat.

MAN IN A BARBERSHOP: Is that bottle of hair tonic any good for growing hair?

BARBER: Good? Why, just the other morning, I spilled some of it on my comb—and today it's a brush.

LYNN: What's a ghost's favorite body of water?

RYAN: What?

LYNN: The Eerie Canal.

PATIENT: Doctor, I need help. I can't seem to remember what I'm talking about from one moment to the next.

DOCTOR: How long has this been going on?

PATIENT: How long has what been going on?

Knock, knock.
Who's there?
Amos.
Amos who?
A mosquito bit me.

Knock, knock.
Who's there?
Andy.
Andy who?
Andy bit me again.

TEACHER: If you have five dollars and you ask your
    father for ten dollars more, how much will you
    have?
DANIEL: Five dollars.
TEACHER: I'm afraid you don't know your arithmetic.
DANIEL: I know my arithmetic. I'm afraid you don't
    know my father.

Knock, knock.
Who's there?
Charlotte.
Charlotte who?
Charlotte of mosquitoes this time of year.

TEACHER: Johnny, how many fingers do you have?

JOHNNY: Ten.

TEACHER: And if three were missing, what would you have?

JOHNNY: No more piano lessons.

PAM: So, how do you like being a chimney sweep?

HOWARD: Soots me.

A snail was crossing the road when he was knocked over by a turtle. The snail was rushed to the hospital, and, after he regained consciousness in the emergency room, the doctor on duty asked him what caused the accident.

"I really can't remember," the snail said. "You see, it all happened so fast."

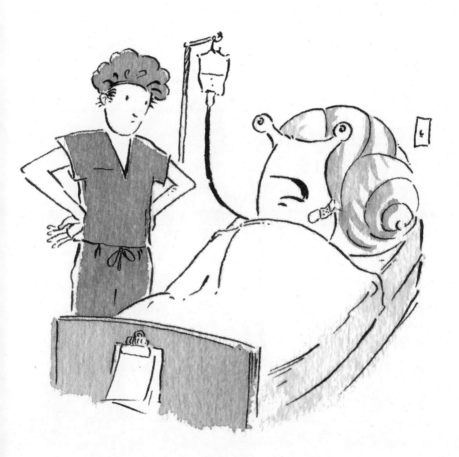

MATTHEW: What did the hat say to the hat rack?
BARBARA: What?
MATTHEW: You stay here and I'll go on ahead.

SCOTT: What happened when the firefly backed into the electric fan?
DENNIS: What?
SCOTT: He was delighted.

JOHN: That ointment the doctor gave me made my arm smart.
JUNE: Why don't you put some on your head?

SON: Dad, how can I get a job as a puppeteer?
DAD: I guess we'll have to pull some strings.

MELVIN: Is it true that both you and your dad were once lion tamers?
ANGELA: Yes, we were.
MELVIN: And did you actually put your hand into a lion's mouth?
ANGELA: Yes, but I did it only once. I was looking for Dad.

The farmer called his rooster Robinson because he crew so.

Some time ago, an American spy was sent to a small town in Ireland to pick up some top-secret documents from a spy with the last name of Murphy. The American's instructions were to walk around town and stop in all the cafés, pubs, and shops until he found him. The American would find the spy by using a special secret phrase that only the spy would recognize.

The American soon found himself on the way to the town. Walking on a deserted country road, he approached a farmer.

"Hello," the American said. "I'm looking for a man named Murphy."

"Well, you have certainly come to the right place," the farmer said. "In the village over the hill, nearly everybody is named Murphy. The owner of the local pub is named Murphy, the schoolteacher is named Murphy, the butcher is named Murphy, and the barber is named Murphy. Indeed, I myself am named Murphy."

Ah! the American agent thought to himself, here's the man I'm looking for. He's disguised as a farmer. So the American said, "The eye of the sun is burning bright over the lakes of Dublin, and the colleens are dancing in the streets."

"Oh," said the farmer. "It is Murphy the spy

you're seeking—he lives ten miles from here in the opposite direction."

Knock, knock.
Who's there?
Gorilla.
Gorilla who?
Gorilla hamburger for me, will you?

Knock, knock.
Who's there?
Dresden.
Dresden who?
Dressden come out to play.

PIANO TUNER: Madam, I've come to tune your piano.
WOMAN AT THE DOOR: But I didn't send for a piano
  tuner.
PIANO TUNER: I know, but your neighbors did.

MOTHER: Doctor, doctor! You have
  to help me. My son thinks
  he's a chicken.
DOCTOR: How long has he
  had this problem?
MOTHER: Oh, about ten
  years now.
DOCTOR: Well, why did
  you wait so long
  before bringing
  him to see
  me?
MOTHER: We
  needed the eggs.

BOXER: Have I done any damage to my opponent yet?
TRAINER: No, but keep swinging. The draft might
give him a cold.

IAN: What do Attila the Hun, Catherine the Great,
and Smokey the Bear have in common?
MATTHEW: They all have the same middle name.

ORRIE: I'm so upset.
HERBERT: Why?
ORRIE: I left my battery-operated radio upstairs.
HERBERT: Don't worry. It'll run down.

SHERLOCK HOLMES: Watson, did you take a bath this
morning?
WATSON: Why, no, Holmes. Is there one missing?

ROBERT: What is green and has four wheels?
DORIS: I give up.
ROBERT: Grass.
DORIS: But grass doesn't have four wheels.
ROBERT: I know. I added that to make it harder.

SAM: I'm a pretty good comedian.
FAYE: Don't make me laugh.

Some folks say that fleas are black,
But I know that it's not so,
Because Mary had a little lamb,
With fleas as white as snow.

NIKKI: My uncle was an efficiency expert, but he
    went too far and he lost his job.
JIMMY: What did he do?
NIKKI: He put unbreakable glass in the fire alarm
    boxes.

JANIE: Why are you standing on your head?
ROSS: Because I lost the belt to my pants.

BARBARA: Matthew, how come your brand-new
    umbrella has a hole in it?
MATTHEW: So I can look up and see when it has
    stopped raining.

KAREN: I've just come from the beauty parlor.
ARNIE: Gee, too bad it was closed.

MATTHEW: What's black and white and red all over,
    and goes up and down, up and down?
MARVIN: What?
MATTHEW: A sunburned zebra on a pogo stick.

JOAN: I would like to take a train to Chicago.

TICKET SELLER: I'm sorry. Only qualified engineers are allowed to drive them.

JOAN: Very well. May I go to Chicago by way of Buffalo?

TICKET SELLER: I'm sorry. None of our buffalo go to Chicago.

JOAN: Just let me have a round-trip ticket.

TICKET SELLER: To where?

JOAN: Back here, of course.

It was a rainy day, and Steve was visiting his friend
Ed and Ed's five-year-old son. Steve noticed that the
child was hammering nails into all the furniture in
the house.

"Why are you allowing your son to drive nails
into all your furniture?" Steve asked his friend.

"Well, it's a rainy day. The kid has nothing to do.
So I told him to go ahead and do it."

"But isn't that expensive?"

"Naah," said Ed. "I get the nails wholesale."

DAVIS: I gave my son a drum for his birthday, and
    now he's going to make me a rich man.
JUDY: By becoming a great drummer?
DAVIS: No, through real estate. I can
    buy my neighbors' houses at
    half price now.

PAUL: What happened
    to the sword
    swallower
    after he went
    on a diet?
NATALIE: He's been
    on pins and nee-
    dles ever since.

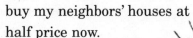

Knock, knock.
Who's there?
Norma Lee.
Norma Lee who?
Normally I don't tell knock-knock jokes.

JOAN: I would like to try on that dress in your store
window.
STORE CLERK: Well, madam, it's all right with us . . .
but you would have more privacy if you used
one of our dressing rooms.

DENNIS: What is yellow and squishy and lives at the
bottom of the sea?
JOAN: What?
DENNIS: A banana with an Aqua-Lung.

SPENCER: What is black and wrinkled and makes pit
stops?
NATALIE: I give up. What?
SPENCER: A hot-rod prune.

MAN IN A RESTAURANT: I'll have two lamb chops. And
please make them lean.
WAITER: Make them lean? The chef will be lucky if
he can get them to stand up.

A woman wanted to travel to Japan for her vacation, so she called the State Department in Washington, D.C., to get information about passports, visas, and inoculations. A clerk told the woman that she would need a passport with a recent photograph.

"Is a cholera shot necessary?" the woman asked.

"No, a black-and-white shot is perfectly acceptable," the clerk replied.

TED: Shall I tell you the new joke about the jump rope?

TOBEY: Naah. Skip it.

CUSTOMER: Waiter, do you serve crabs here?

WAITER: Certainly, sir. We serve everybody.

A man entered a restaurant and sat down. "I would like a ginger ale," he told the waiter.

"Pale?" the waiter asked.

"No. Just a glass."

ANGRY CUSTOMER: I can't eat this food. Call the manager!

WAITER: It won't do any good. He won't eat it, either.

There were two men who were rivals in everything they did—tennis, golf, swimming, everything. One day they decide to go skydiving together. High up over the earth, they jump out of the plane. After falling for about half a mile, the first man pulls the cord on his parachute, but his parachute doesn't open. His backup chute doesn't open either. The second man sees his friend falling to earth. He tears off both his parachutes and shouts, "So you want to race, huh? Okay, let's race!"

TRISTAN: Which way did the computer go?
LAURIE: He went data way.

JOHN: I understand that your aunt Betsy got
    married yesterday.
TRUDY: Yes, she did. But I don't think the marriage
    will last.
JOHN: What makes you say that?
TRUDY: Because when the groom said, "I do," my
    aunt Betsy turned to him and snapped, "Don't
    take that tone of voice with me!"

There was a restaurant that was famous throughout the world for being able to make any kind of sandwich its customers ordered. The owner of the restaurant, in fact, made a standing offer to pay $5,000 to any customer who ordered a sandwich the restaurant could not supply.

One day a man entered the restaurant, sat down at the table, and studied the menu. When he saw the standing offer of $5,000, his eyes lit up. Aha! he thought to himself. I can order a sandwich the restaurant can't make. He called the waiter over to the table. "Waiter, today I would like an elephant-ear sandwich, smothered in penguin tongues, covered with Jamaican hot sauce on white bread."

The waiter took the order and disappeared into the kitchen. Ten minutes passed, then twenty. Still no sandwich. Finally the waiter returned and handed the man a check for $5,000. "We're very sorry, sir," the waiter said, "but we cannot make your sandwich."

"Which of the ingredients don't you have?" the delighted customer asked. "Elephant ears, penguin tongues, or Jamaican hot sauce?"

"We have all of those, sir," the waiter replied. "We just don't have any white bread."

PATIENT: Doctor, my stomach aches. I think it's from the clams I ate.

DOCTOR: Well, did the clams look fresh when you took them out of the shell?

PATIENT: What do you mean, "out of the shell"?

COMEDIAN: I bet I can make a joke on any subject you name.

GIRL IN AUDIENCE: Make a joke about the king.

COMEDIAN: I'm sorry, the king is not a subject.

CUSTOMER IN RESTAURANT: Waiter, there's a twig in my soup.

WAITER: I'm sorry, madam. I'll call the branch manager.

PIANO TEACHER: Your daughter plays the piano like lightning.

MOTHER: You mean she plays so fast?

PIANO TEACHER: No. I mean she never strikes the same place twice.

CUSTOMER: Pardon me. Do you have any wild rice?

WAITER: No, sir. But we can take some tame rice and make it angry.

ARMY PRIVATE #1: It says on the menu "cold boiled chicken." What does that mean?

ARMY PRIVATE #2: Don't be stupid. It means chicken boiled in cold water.

FRANCESCA: The trouble with clocks is that they're so shy.

DAVID: What makes you say that?

FRANCESCA: Because all day long they keep their hands in front of their faces.

NATALIE: What is purple and over 5,000 miles long?
SPENCER: What?
NATALIE: The grape wall of China.

RICHARD: What is the color of a hiccup?
NORA: What?
RICHARD: Burple.

ARLEN: What did one lit birthday candle say to the other?
MOLLY: What?
ARLEN: Are you going out tonight?

SPENCER: Why were the suspenders in jail?
STUART: Why?
SPENCER: They held up a pair of pants.

"You are definitely the puniest, most insignificant thing I have ever laid eyes on," said the elephant to the mouse.

"Let me write that down," the mouse replied. "There's a flea I want to tell it to."

MOTHER: It's Saturday. Why did you wake up so early?
CHILD: I just ran out of sleep.

WOMAN IN RESTAURANT: Waiter, is there soup on
today's menu?
WAITER: There was, but I wiped it off.

ALEX: What do they call four bullfighters in
quicksand?
DANA: I give up.
ALEX: *Cuatro cinco* (sink-oh).

MAUDE: Whenever I'm down in the dumps, I buy a new hat.

MATILDA: Oh, so that's where you get them.

MARYHELEN: What is brown, hairy, and wears sunglasses?

CAROLINE: What?

MARYHELEN: A coconut on vacation.

RICHARD: Could you go behind the car and see if the turn signal is working?

CONNIE: Yes. No. Yes. No. Yes. No. Yes.

ONE WORM TO ANOTHER: Those early risers are for the birds.

JEFF: What has feathers, a bill,
   goes *quack quack quack*, and
   is twenty feet high?
JENNY: A duck on stilts.

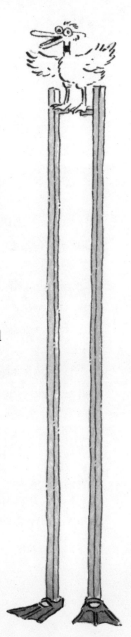

TONI: My grandfather has a problem.
LESLIE: Is that so?
TONI: That's right. He can't make up
   his mind whether to buy a cow or
   a bicycle.
LESLIE: Your grandfather would look
   pretty silly riding a cow.
TONI: That's true. But he'd look a lot
   sillier trying to milk a bicycle.

After running over a rooster that had
been crossing the road, the motorist
stopped his car at a nearby farm-
house to find the rooster's owner.
Seeing the farmer, the motorist
rushed over to him and said, "I'm
very, very sorry. I've just run over
your rooster, but I want you to know
that I'm prepared to replace him."

"Okay," said the farmer. "Let's
hear you crow."

FROG #1: I think I need glasses.
FROG #2: So go see the hoptician.

A man was dining at a fancy restaurant, and he saw the word *escargots* on the menu.

"*Escargots*? What are those?" the man asked his wife.

His wife shook her head. "*Escargots* is French for snails," she told him.

"Well, how would I know?" he replied. "I only eat fast food."

IAN: Come quick, my brother just fell into the mud up to his ankles!
ALEX: Why doesn't he just walk out?
IAN: Because he fell in head first.

ERIC: Why did you sell your water skis?
ZACHARY: Because I couldn't find a lake on a slope.

DANA: What did Dad say when he saw that you'd
    dented his brand-new car?
JAY: Shall I leave out the swear words?
DANA: Of course.
JAY: Well, in that case, he didn't say a thing.

A man was lying down on the main street of a small town, his ear pressed against the pavement. A woman noticed the man and walked over to him. "What are you doing?" she asked.

The man answered. "A black-and-white Buick. A woman is driving. She has four children. Two in the front seat and two in the back. The car has Indiana license plates."

The woman was astonished. "You mean you can tell all that simply by placing your ear to the road?"

"Placing my ear to the road, nothing. I'm talking about the car that ran over me half an hour ago."

It was a dark and stormy night, with thunder and lightning all around. A knight from King Arthur's Round Table entered an inn. His armor was dripping water from head to toe. "Could you please help me?" he asked the innkeeper. "My horse has gone lame, and I must deliver a message to Camelot."

"I'm sorry, gentle knight, but I have no horse at all to offer you," the innkeeper said.

The knight glanced around the room and saw a huge Great Dane lying in front of the fireplace. "That Great Dane looks big enough to ride. Let me ride him to King Arthur's castle. I shall be happy to pay you."

"Oh no," said the innkeeper. "I wouldn't send a knight out on a dog like this."

TEACHER: Mary, why did you miss school yesterday?
MARY: Miss school? Why, I didn't miss it at all.

A wealthy woman, emerging from her Manhattan apartment building, turned to the doorman and said quite haughtily, "Young man, call me a taxi."

"Okay, lady," said the doorman, "you're a taxi."

ANGELA: What do ghosts eat for dessert?
VIN: What?
ANGELA: Ghoul Scout cookies.

AGNES: Well, Joe, is your cold any better?
JOE: Nope.
AGNES: Why don't you drink some orange juice after
     a hot bath?
JOE: I tried that once.
AGNES: What happened?
JOE: After I drank the hot bath, I couldn't get the
     orange juice down.